WEDDING VOWS

How to express your love in your own words

by
PEG KEHRET

photography by

Meriwether Publishing Ltd., Publisher
P.O. Box 7710
Colorado Springs, CO 80933

Editor: Arthur Zapel
Typesetting: Sharon Garlock
Cover design: Michelle Z. Gallardo

© Copyright MCMLXXXIX Meriwether Publishing Ltd.
Printed in the United States of America
First Edition

Library of Congress Cataloging-in-Publication Data

Kehret, Peg.
    Wedding vows : how to express your love in your own words / by Peg Kehret.
        p.   cm.
     ISBN 0-916260-59-3
    √ 1. Marriage service.   √ I. Title.
HQ745.K44   1989
      392.5 -- dc20

                                      89-32089
                                      CIP

For Carl

TABLE OF CONTENTS

Introduction

The Most Important Event of Your Life

When you get married, you change your life. Marriage is the most intimate relationship there is and the decision to marry is the biggest commitment most people ever make.

Because getting married is such a significant step, most people say their wedding day is the most important and meaningful day of their life. Decades later, the wedding day stands out clearly in the memory of both bride and groom.

Throughout history, weddings have been times of celebration. Families and friends gather to witness the wedding and to heap blessings on the couple. There are ceremonies, traditions, feasts. Dozens of details must be arranged. There are florists to consult, rings to buy, food to prepare. A marriage license must be obtained, invitations printed, and music selected.

In the midst of all this planning, it is easy to lose sight of the most vital part of the wedding day — the actual exchange of vows.

The Most Important Part of the Wedding

The exchange of vows is the heart of the wedding ceremony. All of the rest — music, flowers, blessings from the officiate — are lovely accompaniments. But it is the vows, the promises that the bride and groom make to each other, which constitute the most important part of the wedding.

Technically, the exchange of vows *is* the wedding. The moment when the vows are spoken is the moment of covenant; the vows are the words which serve to join a couple in marriage. The bride and groom could stand with an officiate, repeat only the vows, and be declared married. On the other hand, they could have a thrilling organ processional, bridesmaids, ushers, flowers, a Bible reading, some poetry, a beautiful solo, a brief sermon, a kiss, and a recessional — and still *not* be married. Without the vows, all of these other trappings mean nothing. The vows are the heart of every wedding service. Without them, all the rest is pointless.

Most couples would not dream of going to their own wedding without knowing exactly what they will wear. Hours are devoted to coordinating the colors of the flowers and the napkins. Surely the wedding vows deserve at least as much consideration as these less important matters.

No intelligent person would sign a legal document without reading it first. Yet hundreds of couples never know what vows they will be making until it's time to make them. They know all about the bridesmaid's shoes and the frosting on the cake — but they don't know what they will be promising to do for the rest of their lives. They hear their wedding vows for the first time when they're standing before a crowd of witnesses on their wedding day. Often they repeat vows which were written decades before they were born.

If the ceremony is recorded, they may hear it many times in the years ahead and will regret that they did not write or choose their own personal vows. Surely the most significant words of a lifetime should be a meaningful expression of their love for each other.

A Love Like No Other

There has never been a love quite like yours. Let the vows you make during your wedding ceremony reveal the unique love you share.

Since it is the vows which make a wedding ceremony most meaningful and memorable, they should be discussed and decided upon well in advance. Give them the thought they deserve.

By writing your own wedding vows, or thoughtfully selecting one of the original vows in this book, you make sure that your wedding ceremony reflects who you are, how you feel toward each other, and what you hope your marriage will be.

Chapter One

How to Use
this Book

What This Book Can Do for You

If you plan to be married, this book can help you decide exactly how you want to pledge your love. It will help you put into words what is most important about your relationship. It will show you how to express your love in a way that is beautiful and special.

This book is not a general wedding guide. It won't tell you how far in advance of the ceremony the invitations should be mailed or which musical selections are appropriate for a recessional. There is no check list for when to order mints, nuts, napkins or punch. Dozens of other resources are available to help you plan such details.

This book focuses only on the actual wedding vows. It contains more than sixty original promises, pledges, and declarations of love which are intended to be used as a part of any religious or civil wedding ceremony. These examples were written for a wide variety of couples and are designed to fit into many different types of weddings.

There is also a chapter of Anniversary Vows for couples who want to celebrate an anniversary by renewing their commitment in a special way.

The sample wedding vows are not complete marriage ceremonies. They are the promises exchanged by bride and groom, and are meant to be used in conjunction with any church or secular service.

No matter what your age, background, or situation in life, there will almost certainly be several examples that will suit you. The instructions will show you how to use only the parts of the vows which have most meaning for you and how to adapt them so that they are uniquely your own.

Whether you plan a traditional church wedding, an informal home or garden wedding, or a wedding that's completely different from any ever done before, you will be able, with this book, to tailor your wedding vows to fit the occasion.

When the book, *Vows of Love and Marriage,* by Peg Kehret, was first published, it received praise from critics and the public. Many of the original vows in that book proved to be so popular that they are included here. They have been used, either whole or in part, by countless brides and grooms.

Along with these specific examples, this book gives you step-by-step instructions for writing your own personal wedding vows. It will show you how to decide what phrases are most important to you and how to use them most effectively.

This technique for writing your own wedding vows has been used successfully many times. Even couples who think they don't have "a way with words" or who feel they lack sufficient writing skills to take on a project of such importance, have been able to write their own wedding vows, using the method and examples contained here.

All the information you need to write your own vows is in this book. You won't have to make numerous trips to the library or struggle through volumes of poetry and quotations. That background work has already been done for you. All you need to do is read and discuss the vows in this book and follow the instructions for using them. The result will be wedding vows which are personal, meaningful and uniquely your own.

Read This Book Together

This book is for couples. Both the bride and the groom should read it, preferably together. It will provide the basis for discussions, not only about what you want your wedding vows to be but also what you want your marriage to be. Because the vows are the most personal part of the wedding ceremony, they touch on those matters which are dearest to each of you.

One immediate benefit of writing your own vows is that you will think together about the goals you will work toward in your life together and about what you value most in your relationship. The act of writing your vows will help you understand exactly what kind of long-range commitment you are about to make. It's a way to explore together your deepest hopes for this union, a way to share your dreams of the future.

The result of such discussions will be threefold. First, you will have a better understanding of what the impending marriage means to both of you. Second, you will grow closer because you are discussing matters which are vitally important to you. And last, when your wedding day arrives, the ceremony will have far greater meaning for you because you played an active part in creating and personalizing it.

Writing your vows together can also be a way to uncover potential problems. One bride-to-be wanted to include this phrase in her vows: "I take you to be my husband and the father of my children." Her future groom was aghast; he had no desire to have any children.

The discussion which ensued was crucial and it was important to have it *before* the wedding.

Although most brides and grooms have already talked about whether or not to have a family, the selection of what to include in their wedding vows often opens the door to discussions about their most cherished hopes of what this marriage will be. Deciding what promises to make can help you know what you expect of each other.

If you know what you want out of your marriage,

you also know what you must put into it. Writing your vows together will help you start your marriage with understanding and commitment.

Take Your Time

This book should not be skimmed in a hurry. Read it slowly and thoughtfully. Evaluate each of the vows and decide what you like or don't like about it. Think about them. Talk it over.

You will eliminate some vows immediately. Others will make you pause and say, "Yes. Yes! That's exactly how I feel." It is those phrases which you should try to include in your own ceremony.

Chapter Two

The Officiate

Choosing the Officiate

Someone — minister, rabbi, judge or other person with the authority to make your marriage legal — will have to preside at your wedding. If you plan to be married in a church, the minister or other officiate of that church will usually conduct the wedding service.

If you have no religious affiliation or if you prefer not to have a church wedding, you will need to find someone to perform the duties of officiate.

Whether this is someone you know or someone you select only for this occasion, be sure to choose a person who will conduct the service according to your wishes.

Tell the Officiate Your Plans

Consult early with the officiate about your plan to write your own vows. Most officiates have a standard wedding ceremony that they use so you will need to inform him or her of your intention to write your vows yourselves.

He will probably be enthusiastic about your plans and may even have copies of other original ceremonies which he can share with you and which may give you additional ideas for your own service.

If it's a church wedding, the officiate will almost

certainly want to see a copy of what you plan to say. He needs to be sure that it is appropriate and that it contains nothing which goes against the teachings of that particular church. Don't wait until the last minute to show him what you want to do. If there's any difference of opinion, it's much easier to deal with it while you have plenty of time to make changes.

Very rarely, a minister will refuse to allow a bride and groom to make any changes in the standard ceremony. In such cases, it's necessary to decide whether your desire to personalize your wedding is strong enough to merit changing the ceremony to a different location.

Fortunately, most officiates welcome the chance to marry couples who are willing to put time and effort into creating a personal and meaningful wedding.

Find Out What the Officiate Plans to Say

Ask the minister or other officiate to give you a copy of any remarks he intends to make during the service. Get this several days in advance of the wedding so that there's ample time to make changes and correct misconceptions.

By writing your own vows and sharing them with the officiate ahead of time, you will probably prevent the disaster of having the ceremony contain phrases or philosophies with which you do not agree. But don't take chances. Make sure what the officiate plans to say.

Failing to do so can result in misfortune. One woman, divorced after a brief teenage marriage, eventually married again. Since the groom had not been married before, his family urged them to have a large wedding and she went along with the plans.

Neither the bride nor the groom had a home church so the wedding was held in a rented hall. A neighbor of the groom's parents was a minister and, although he did not know either the bride or the groom, he agreed to officiate at the ceremony. Unfortunately, no one thought to ask him what he planned to say during his part of the service.

When the wedding day arrived, the bride and groom stood happily before a large gathering of friends and family. The minister opened the service by saying that marriage is a sacred lifetime covenant with God. "A man or woman who breaks the marriage vows through divorce and then remarries," he declared, "is living in sin."

Family and friends, knowing that the bride had been married before, were extremely uncomfortable. The groom was furious, and the horrified bride felt demeaned and shamed. What should have been a joyous occasion became a painful ordeal.

Another woman, an attorney who was head of her own law firm, was startled to hear the minister at her wedding declare that the husband was responsible for all family decisions and the wife was expected to trust his judgment. At that moment the bride was faced with a no-win choice: she could either pretend to agree, and promise something which she didn't believe, or she could interrupt her own wedding and challenge the officiate, thereby distracting all thoughts from the marriage ceremony and turning her wedding into an argument for women's equality.

She chose not to make a scene and didn't dispute the minister's words, but later she regretted her decision. By agreeing to a statement which she found personally repugnant, she felt she had cheapened herself and diminished the beauty of the rest of the ceremony.

Don't leave yourself open to such unhappy surprises. Find out what the officiate plans to say.

In recent years, many couples have objected to services which declare that the husband is head of the household and the wife is subservient to him. If such comments are part of the usual wedding service in the church where your wedding will be held, be sure that you fully agree with this philosophy before allowing it to be included in your special day.

By asking to see a copy of the officiate's remarks in advance, you can prevent uncomfortable and unnecessary shocks.

Chapter Three

What to Include in
Your Wedding Vows

Legal Requirements for Wedding Vows

There are no phrases which *must* be included in your vows in order for the marriage ceremony to be legal. As long as the bride and groom have a marriage license, two witnesses to sign the certificate, an officiate who is licensed by the state to perform weddings and, in some states, a blood test, their marriage will be legal no matter what they say. You can stand in total silence if you choose and you'll end up just as married.

While personal vows and promises may not be legally necessary in order for the marriage to be valid, they are important if the ceremony is to be a loving reflection of the two people involved.

Something Old, Something New

Just because you want to personalize your wedding vows doesn't mean you can't use any of the familiar, customary language. It's perfectly acceptable to use a blend of old and new. It can be satisfying to use some of the well-known phrases which our society has long associated with weddings. They provide the ceremony with roots that go deep. People in the audience will hear such tradtional phrases and remember other weddings — perhaps their own.

These phrases may have special memories for the

bride and groom, too. Maybe a brother or sister had an especially beautiful wedding, or one of you may have participated in the wedding of a dear friend. Such memories lend a feeling of continuity to the occasion, a sense that this couple, while unique and separate, is still part of society and is carrying on that society's most cherished traditions.

Many people feel secure and comfortable with certain words and phrases that have passed down through the generations. If you feel that way about parts of a traditional ceremony, you should include those parts in your wedding. Never be different just for the sake of being different. Be different only to be better.

One woman, Susan B., felt especially fond of the Protestant ceremony in which the minister says, "*(Name)*, wilt thou have this woman to be thy wedded wife, to live together after God's ordinance in the holy estate of matrimony? Wilt thou love her, comfort her, honor and keep her in sickness and in health; and, forsaking all others, keep thee only unto her, so long as you both shall live?"

The same questions are asked of the bride. Both bride and groom respond, "I will."

Susan had been the maid of honor when her older sister married. She remembered the thrill she felt when she heard her sister and brother-in-law repeat their vows. She wanted to include those same vows in her own wedding. At the same time, she wanted something more individual, something particularly her own. Her fiance, too, wanted their vows to be unique.

Their solution was to use both. Susan and her husband repeated the traditional vows — and then they gave their own wedding vows, which they wrote themselves.

Out-Dated Phrases

If you decide to use all or part of any traditional vows, be sure you completely understand all the wording. Many wedding services contain language which is no longer relevant or even understandable.

For example, some religious wedding ceremonies

contain the words, "I promise to love and sustain you in the bonds of marriage." That phrase is frequently misunderstood.

The word "bond" has several meanings, some positive, some negative. It can mean something that binds or restrains, such as a fetter. (Slaves were held in bondage — not a constructive way to look at marriage.) As used in wedding services, bond means to adhere firmly — a more positive interpretation. Still, the word "bond" has many common meanings which have nothing at all to do with marriage. *Webster's New Collegiate Dictionary* lists one of the meanings as, "a 100-proof straight whiskey that has been aged at least four years under government supervision before being bottled." One bride-to-be confessed that she thought the bonds of marriage were some sort of financial obligation.

A few other phrases are sometimes included in wedding ceremonies even though they are out-dated or even objectionable. In earlier times, the phrase "man and wife", was commonly used. "Husband and wife" seems more equal.

The question, "Who gives this woman to be married to this man?" used to be a part of many weddings. Today, few people think anyone has the right to give away another person.

Some early ceremonies contain references to procreation which make it sound as if the sole reason for getting married is to have children. Few couples today, even those who desire a family, believe that children are the only goal of their union.

If you encounter such phrases in the ceremony suggested by your church or your officiate, you don't have to use them. Just because certain words are usually included in a ceremony, does not mean they are right for you. Remember, the wedding vows can be whatever you want them to be and the marriage will still be legal.

Wedding ceremonies can be traced back through history. The occasion is important partly because weddings have been significant occurrences for so many years, in all societies. Nevertheless, *this* wedding has never happened before. It is a unique, once-only event and as such it should reflect your personal tastes and feelings, regardless of what other people have done in the past.

Think Positive

Positive phrases seem more appropriate to such a joyous occasion than negative ones. When writing and revising your promises, try to think of ways to say them in a positive fashion. For example, in many traditional wedding services, the bride and groom promise to love each other, "until death do us part." Even contemporary versions of the traditional ceremony say, "until we are parted by death." For most people, the word "death" has negative connotations. It is not a happy word. Instead of promising to love each other until you are parted by death, you could promise to love, "for all the days of my life" or "as long as I live." The meaning of the words is basically the same — you are still promising to love each other for the rest of your lives. But by phrasing your words in a positive fashion, you make your exchange of vows happier.

Negative: I will love you until I die.
Positive: I will love you for all of my life.

Negative: I promise never to be unfaithful to you.
Positive: I promise always to be faithful to you.

Negative: No one else will ever be as important to me as you are.
Positive: You will always be the most important person to me.

Expect Your Marriage to Last

Some couples try to hedge their bets by writing vows which allow them an escape if the marriage doesn't last. For example, they promise to stay together, "as long as we both shall love."

One couple wanted to promise to love each other "for the length of the marriage." The clergyman who was doing the ceremony wisely talked them out of that phrase.

Although the high divorce rate is, sadly, a well-known statistic, a wedding ceremony is no place for un-certainty. A bride or groom who suspects the marriage might not work would be wise to postpone the wedding until all doubts are gone.

Realistically, even marriages which begin with high hopes and deep love sometimes fall apart. But why anticipate the worst? Instead, anticipate the best. Assume your marriage will be a solid, joyful, enduring union.

If there's anything to the theory of self-fulfilling prophecy, why not expect happiness?

No Jokes

Joyous is not the same as silly. While you are writing your vows, you'll probably think of at least one joke such as, "I promise never to interrupt when you're watching a football game," or, "I promise to make strawberry waffles for breakfast at least once a week."

Have your laughs together while you're brainstorming for ideas, but don't include them in the final version. Such frivolous statements devalue a wedding ceremony. You might get a chuckle from the wedding guests with such statements but the laughter will make the entire ceremony seem less important.

Your wedding vows should reflect your finest thoughts and express your most cherished dreams. This isn't the time for cheap laughs.

Keep that in mind when you decide on the wording of your vows. "I promise always to be honest with you," is a valid statement, worthy of your wedding. "I promise never to hide my MasterCard℠ bill from you," is trite and not acceptable. Both sentences deal with the matter of honesty but the first one does it in a way that speaks to noble intentions while the second one focuses on a petty, mundane matter. Your wedding should be a time of lofty ideals and fine intentions. Be noble.

Please Don't Preach

Your wedding is not the time to expound on your personal religious beliefs. Naturally, your faith will be an integral part of the ceremony. A Christian wedding, a Jewish wedding, a Buddhist wedding, or any other religious marriage ceremony will include references to the faith of the bride and groom. It's appropriate for any religious ceremony to include a prayer or a reading which has special meaning to people of that faith.

But don't preach a sermon and don't allow the officiate to preach one, either. A wedding is not the place to attempt religious conversions. Your guests will probably be of varying spiritual beliefs and it is inconsiderate to make them feel uncomfortable. Let your wedding service reflect your own beliefs without trying to force others to accept them.

A wedding is the celebration of the love between a man and a woman. Guests of all faiths should feel elated by the ceremony.

Let Your Emotions Show

Most of us have been conditioned since childhood to keep our innermost feelings hidden. It can be difficult to express privately what you feel for each other, and even harder to divulge your love in public.

This is the time to let your emotions show. Your wedding vows should be intimate, significant expressions of your love. A wedding is the one occasion when most people dare to be openly sentimental. Do not be afraid, when writing your vows, to be candid about your feelings. On that day of days, no one will scoff if you speak honestly about the depth of your love. By publicly acknowledging your deepest feelings, you give your partner a beautiful memory. Friends and family who witness such expressions of love will feel uplifted, and honored that they were able to share in the event.

Participation by Friends and Family

Another way to personalize your wedding ceremony is to give people who are important to you an active part in the service. Perhaps a family member or close friend could be asked to give a prayer or a reading. If this is done, the material used can be customized, making it a unique and special part of the ceremony.

You can also give a more personal feeling to some traditional parts of a service by having special people participate. For example, ask the bride's aunt or uncle to read the Scripture. Or have the groom's grandfather or a dear friend read the officiate's part of a responsive reading.

It's best to ask such people to assist with something they will read. Don't expect them to memorize a poem or to speak in any other way from memory. It's an honor to be asked to participate in a wedding but you want the honored person to enjoy the occasion. Most people would not feel comfortable "performing" from memory and would worry too much about making a mistake that would detract from the beauty of the ceremony.

Don't put your favorite people on the spot. If you ask someone to take a part in the wedding ceremony, make it clear that they don't have to say yes. Allow them the privilege of declining without feeling that they are letting you down.

Some people truly are not comfortable in front of an audience. If your favorite uncle would rather watch from the safety of a pew, be gracious about accepting his feelings.

Chapter Four

Writing Your Own Vows

Writing Your Own Wedding Vows

It's time now to plan what you will say when you exchange vows with the person you love most. If you follow the guidelines below, one step at a time, the result will be meaningful, personal wedding vows that pledge your love exactly the way you want to say it.

Step One: Read and Discuss the Vows in This Book

The first step in writing your own vows is to read and discuss the vows in Chapters Five, Six, Seven and Eight of this book. Cross out any that you know you won't want to use.

Chapter Five consists of vows in monologue form. They are meant to be spoken by only one person. You might want to choose one of these vows and both use it. One of you would say the words and then the other one would say the same words.

You might prefer to select two different vows, one for the bride and one for the groom.

In Chapter Six, the vows are in dialogue form. With these vows, bride and groom (and, sometimes, the officiate) speak their lines alternately to each other.

Chapter Seven contains special dialogues to use when exchanging wedding rings. Couples who decide to use conventional vows in the rest of the ceremony may still want to use one of these vows when they give and receive their rings.

Chapter Eight includes vows for special circumstances, as well as an Addendum that can be included at the end of any service.

Perhaps you will find one vow which reads as if it were written especially for you. It says what is in your hearts better than you could ever say it yourselves. If that's the case, use it as written. You can then skip to Step Six in this chapter.

If, when you read the vows in Chapters Five, Six, Seven and Eight, you don't find exactly the vows you want, proceed to Step Two in this chapter.

Step Two: Read Again the Vows That Weren't Eliminated

After you have read all of the vows in Chapters Five, Six, Seven and Eight, go back and reread the vows that were not eliminated. There will be some where you like one part of the vow but not another. Mark these, either by crossing out the phrases you don't want or by highlighting the phrases you like.

In some of the vows, there may be only one sentence, or even a part of a sentence, that you like. Eliminate the rest and keep that one small portion for further consideration.

This step of the process is only a matter of keeping the phrases you like best and cutting out everything else.

Step Three: List the Phrases You Like Most

On a fresh sheet of paper, make a list of the sentences or phrases which you like the most. Eliminate until you have no more than ten on your list.

You will probably have parts of several different vows on your list. That's okay. The vows in this book are meant to be the springboard for you to write your own vows.

As you make your list, you may have ideas for different ways to say the sentences you are copying from the book. Go ahead and change them if you want to. Condense these examples or expand them. Revise them any way you want. What is right and true for one couple is not necessarily right and true for another.

If one of these vows suggests a whole new idea that you like, write it down. Don't be afraid to be original. If you decide later that you don't like the new idea, you can always discard it.

One couple, Kathy and Glenn, made this list:

1. *I promise to be a true and loyal friend to you.*

2. *I make this vow gladly.*

3. *I loved you before this ceremony; I love you more because of it.*

4. *I do not expect you to fulfill all my dreams. I ask only that you share them with me.*

5. *A true marriage is not a ceremony. It is an on-going commitment.*

6. *From this day forward, I will walk beside you.*

7. *I promise to keep my heart ever open to you.*

8. *Our joys will be multiplied because we will celebrate together. Our sorrows will be lessened because we will share our burdens with each other.*

9. *I accept you, without reservation, as my husband/wife.*

10. *I will try to be worthy of your love and trust.*

Each of the ten items on Glenn and Kathy's list is from one of the vows published in this book. Your list may be too, or you may have some sentences that are your own ideas.

When your list is complete, read through it several times and select the phrases which are most meaningful to you. Maybe you'll want to keep all ten. Maybe you'll keep only four or five.

Step Four: Experiment With the Order

After you have chosen the sentences and phrases you like best, you must decide what order to put them in. A good way to do this is to cut up your list with scissors so each phrase is on a separate slip of paper. Keep only the phrases you think you want to use. Now rearrange the slips of paper in various ways until you find the order that sounds the best.

When you've decided on a possible order, write all the sentences again but this time write them as one paragraph, just the way the vow would be spoken.

Kathy and Glenn, who compiled the list above, decided to keep only numbers 2, 4, 5, 6, 8 and 10. They rearranged the slips of paper and decided that a logical sequence for these phrases would be: 5, 8, 4, 6, 10. When they wrote the paragraph that way, it read like this:

"A true marriage is not a ceremony but an on-going commitment. Our joys will be multiplied because we will celebrate together. Our sorrows will be lessened because we will share our burdens with each other. I do not expect you to fulfill all my dreams; I ask only that you share them with me. From this day forward, I will walk beside you. I will try to be worthy of your love and trust."

When you have arranged the phrases you like best in what seems like the best order, write them out as a single paragraph, the way Kathy and Glenn did.

Step Five: Revise

After reading this composite vow, you will most likely want to make further changes. If you've used only phrases from this book, you may decide to add something uniquely your own. You may need to eliminate a word or two in order to make the phrases flow more smoothly.

Try using contractions, to give a sentence a more informal tone. Use a thesaurus to find different words with the same meaning. Sometimes substituting such a word will make the phrase sound better to you.

If you like the individual thoughts but aren't sure if the piece sounds good as a whole, ask for help. You probably know someone who is an English teacher, or a librarian, or a journalist. Anyone who works regularly with words should be able to quickly suggest any necessary changes in the structure of your vows.

Here is how Kathy and Glenn rewrote their paragraph:

> *"I believe that marriage is not just a ceremony. It is an on-going commitment. Today I commit myself to you. From now on, we will celebrate together and our celebration will multiply our joys. From now on, we will share our troubles and the burdens we carry will seem lighter. I don't ask you to fulfill all my dreams. I ask only that you share my dreams with me and allow me to share your dreams with you. From this day forward, I will walk beside you, trying always to be worthy of your love."*

Although Glenn and Kathy began with a list of phrases taken from the vows in this book, the vow they said at their wedding was distinctly their own, reflecting their personal feelings of love.

You can do the same. First, read and discuss the vows in this book. Then make a list of the sentences you find most meaningful. Experiment with their order. Revise. Keep trying until you hit on the combination of words that is exactly what you want.

Kathy and Glenn wrote their vow in monologue form. At their wedding, they each said exactly the same words to each other. Glenn spoke first, reading the paragraph that they wrote. Then Kathy read the same paragraph.

If you prefer to do your vows in dialogue form, you will need to break up the single paragraph, alternating lines. For example, this is how Kathy and Glenn's vow might be written in dialogue form:

Bride: I believe that marriage is not just a ceremony. It is an on-going commitment. Today I commit myself to you.

Groom: I also believe marriage is an on-going commitment. Today I commit myself to you.

Bride: From now on, we will celebrate together and our celebrations will multiply our joys.

Groom: From now on, we will share our troubles and the burdens we carry will seem lighter.

Bride: I don't ask you to fulfill all my dreams. I ask only that you share my dreams with me and allow me to share your dreams with you.

Groom: I don't expect you to fulfill all my dreams. I ask only that you share my dreams with me and allow me to share your dreams with you.

Bride: From this day forward, I will walk beside you, trying always to be worthy of your love.

Groom: From this day forward, I will walk beside you, trying always to be worthy of your love.

You might want to try writing your final paragraph both ways, as monologue and as dialogue. Then decide which way you like better.

Step Six: Read Your Vows Out Loud

When you have what you think is the perfect set of wedding vows, read them out loud. Sometimes a sentence will look fine on paper but will be difficult to understand when it's read aloud. Or you might inadvertently include a tongue-twister that's impossible to pronounce clearly. Because your vows will be spoken before witnesses, they should be both meaningful to the heart and beautiful to the ear.

Read your vows out loud and change anything that seems awkward.

Step Seven: Make Copies

When you've decided on the final version of your vows make clear, legible copies of it. Be businesslike at this point. Type or print out the material, double-spaced, with a clear black ribbon. Make enough photocopies so that you each have one, the officiate has one, and any other person who needs to be familiar with the order of service (such as the organist) has one.

Put the officiate's copy in a folder or a three-ring binder. It will be easy to handle and will eliminate the shuffling of papers. It also ensures that no pages will get dropped or lost. Give the officiate his copy several days in advance, even if the material has already been approved. That way, if a different physical arrangement is preferred, such as typing your original vows on the same page as whatever precedes or follows them, there is time for this to be done.

Be sure to put one copy of your vows away with your other treasured possessions. You may want to get it out each year on your anniversary and repeat your vows, as a special reminder of your wedding day. One good place to keep the copy of your vows is in the photo album with your wedding pictures.

Step Eight: Practice

Some couples like to memorize their wedding vows. This is fine if it doesn't make you too nervous. You don't want to spoil your own enjoyment of the ceremony because you're worried that you'll forget your lines. If you have ever had to give a speech, you know how easy it is to go blank at the crucial moment.

If you decide to speak from memory, give the officiate a copy of your vows, just in case. That way, if your memory fails, you can always read your vows. Or the officiate can read them, and you can repeat the words after him. The thought and meaning will be just as beautiful, and just as personal, when the words are read.

Whether you plan to speak from memory or to read your vows, practice them out loud several times. You need to be completely familiar with the words. If you are using one of the vows in dialogue form, it's important to practice together so that you both feel comfortable with the timing.

The vows will seem even more special when you repeat them on your wedding day if you are completely familiar with them. And you will be more relaxed if you have rehearsed together several times.

If you have more than one page, number the pages.

Put your copies of your vows in a folder or a book. Hands have been known to tremble during weddings and it is much easier to read from a paper that's supported by a folder or book than from a single sheet of paper.

Some people like to put their vows in a Bible. You may want to use a book from which you've selected a reading for your ceremony or perhaps a book which has been particularly meaningful to you as you've evolved your personal philosophy. A plain white folder, the kind that has prongs which protrude through the paper to hold it in place, will also work nicely.

Step Nine: Speak Up!

When *THE* day arrives and it's time to speak your vows, face each other, not the officiate. Your vows are for you, and you should look at each other as you give them. Speak loudly and clearly so that all of your wedding guests can hear. Most of all, speak always with love, for the most beloved person you will ever know will remember your words for the rest of his or her life.

Promises and
Declarations of Love
(Vows in Monologue Form)

I take your hand in mine. This symbolizes friendship and I promise now to be your true and loyal friend.

It symbolizes union and I promise to keep our union uppermost in my life.

It symbolizes help and caring. I promise to help you whenever and however you need me.

Most of all, it symbolizes love, and love is what I feel for you.

I take your hand in mine — for this hour, for this day, for this lifetime.

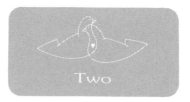

Today is a day of memories. We remember our childhoods. We remember, with gratitude, all that our parents did to prepare us to lead independent and useful lives.

We remember the day we met and our first date and our courtship.

Now we begin to build new memories. From this day on, our memories will be not of you and of me, but of us.

I promise to do all that I can to make your future memories happy ones.

Three

I want to tell you some of the reasons why I love you.

I love you because you are gentle. In a world full of violence, you dare to be tender. You aren't ashamed to cry and you have empathy for all living creatures.

I love you because you are optimistic. You always look for the positive and overlook the negative.

I love you because you are fun to be with. You see the humor in life and your laughter brings smiles to everyone around.

I love you because you are loyal. I can trust you to keep my secrets. You never speak ill of a friend.

I love you because you believe in me and your belief helps me achieve more than I ever could otherwise.

I love you because you accept me as I am. With you, I can be completely myself.

I will try, in every way possible, to make you as happy as you make me.

I do not speak easily of love. Especially before an audience. Love is private and personal.

But today I declare myself in public. I announce my feelings to our families and friends. In front of all the people who are most important to both of us, I say, "I love you, (name)."

Because a public promise seems somehow more important and more binding than a private one, I want all of these witnesses to hear it.

I promise to do all in my power to keep our love as fresh and strong as it is today. I will be faithful to you, both with my body and in my mind. I will try always to put the good of our marriage first in my life.

In a life filled with happiness, this is my happiest day.

From this day on, our lives are intertwined. I will do all that I can to shield you from hurt and disappointment.

I do not expect you to meet all of my needs. Rather, I will meet my own needs so that I am a whole person, willing to share my life.

I will nurture you when you need care. I will cheer for you when you attempt new endeavors. I will believe in you when others may doubt.

Most of all, I will love you — for today and for all of our tomorrows.

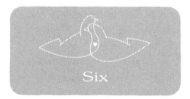

I will try always to make you proud of me.

I will care for my body so that my good health will be an asset to our relationship. I will strive for intellectual growth so that I'll be an interesting companion.

You are special to me in a way that no one has ever been before. It is this uniqueness which I cherish above all else.

Your faith in me gives me faith in myself. Your pleasure in me gives me confidence. Your love for me gives me a joy deeper than I imagined possible.

I promise that I will try in every way to be worthy of your love.

Seven

We are soul mates. A love this strong cannot be bound by the limitations of our physical bodies and will endure even separation by death.

I do not pledge my love until death do us part. I pledge it for all eternity because I believe that you and I will be together always.

I make this vow gladly, confident that our love is strong enough to bind us together even if we should be separated physically.

I pledge my love for you throughout this lifetime and for all the unknown, unseen lifetimes to come. Wherever or whomever we may be in the future, I will love you.

We have been together before — we are together now — we will be together always.

Eight

We are surrounded today by the music of love. We know not what discords may lie around the corner of next year but whatever they may be, love's harmony will overpower them.

When I look at you, my heart sings and the most mundane phrases seem like lyrical masterpieces.

You are the melody of my life; the theme which runs through all that I see or hear or do.

We are surrounded today by the music of love. May it be only a prelude to the loving harmony of our life together.

Nine

I come gladly to this moment. We have already shared much of our lives and we know from experience that we get along well together.

Although we have lived together, it has not been enough.

Today I choose to make a deeper commitment to you, a legal and binding contract. It is my way of telling you that our experience together has been so good that I want it to continue for the rest of my life.

I loved you before this ceremony. I love you more because of it.

I promise to share with you the good times — the evenings that are free of obligations, the holidays, the vacations.

I promise to share the bad times, too — the disappointments and hurts, the secret fears.

I will trust you with my dreams and I vow never to make fun of yours. I will try to be supportive of whatever brings you fulfillment.

I will put your feelings above all others. Our time together will be important to me.

I know I'm not perfect and I'll make allowances for your imperfections.

I promise always to be honest with you.

I have never loved anyone but you. You are my first love and my last.

I loved you the first time we met and I will love you always. You are everything I ever hoped to find in a partner.

I promise to be faithful to you in thought, word, and deed. I will never knowingly deceive you or hurt you.

I want to spend the rest of my life with you and I promise to be the best person I can be so that our lifetime together will be one of happiness and growth.

Today is my lucky day.

I am lucky that I met you and lucky that you agreed to marry me. I promise to love you and care for you. I promise to share my worldly goods, my time, my home — all of my life with you.

I promise to do everything I can to make you feel lucky, too.

Today is a new beginning. We are leaving behind our past lives and starting our new life together. I will leave behind as well any preconceived ideas of how you should act.

I want our marriage to be a partnership in every way. I promise to share with you the small daily pleasures and chores, as well as the excitement of stimulating ideas.

I want for you that which brings you the greatest personal fulfillment. I promise to encourage and support you as you strive to attain the finest of which you are capable.

I expect to be a better person because of this marriage. I hope you will be a better person because of this marriage, too.

Fourteen

Once only comes true love. Once only comes a feeling so strong and sure that it is an invisible lifeline between two souls.

True love is demonstrated when each partner puts the loved one's happiness above all else. In true love, the permanent good of the partnership is more important than any temporary pleasure. True love manifests itself through loyalty, concern and faith in the other person's integrity.

Once only comes true love. Through you, it has come to me.

Fifteen

When problems seem overwhelming, I think of you and I gain confidence. When secret, nighttime terrors shatter my peace of mind, I remember you and I am calmed. When I'm lonely, I need only ask, and you are there.

You give purpose to my days and joyous comfort to my nights. You are my reason for being.

I offer you today the one gift that I give to no one else: I offer you my love.

Sixteen

(*Name*), I have spent many hours searching for the right way to say what is in my heart today. I've read poems and prose and thumbed through books of quotations.

I tried to describe my feelings for you in a dozen different ways but no matter how I expressed myself, it seemed inadequate.

There are no words deep enough, meaningful enough and exciting enough to verbalize what I feel.

And so, for lack of a better way, I will use the simplest expression of all.

I love you.

Seventeen

(*Name*), I take you now to be my (*husband/wife*). I promise to live with you, to trust you and to cherish you. I will love you when we are apart as well as when we are together. I will love you in sickness and in health, in good times and in bad.

I will work with you toward our common goals and share our leisure joyfully.

I pledge myself now to be ever faithful to you with my body, my mind and my heart.

Please accept my love.

Eighteen

When I was a child, I read a lot of fairy tales. In these stories, the hero and heroine discovered their love for each other, rode off into the sunset, and "lived happily ever after."

As I child, I accepted the premise that, because they were in love, they would always be happy. I also accepted pumpkins changing into coaches.

Now I know that no other person, no matter how beloved, can be responsible for making me happy. Happiness must come from within.

I do not think that because we are together we'll never have any problems but I believe that because we love each other we can solve whatever problems come along.

For Cinderella and Prince Charming, their wedding day was the end of the story. For us, it is only the beginning.

Nineteen

Marriage is not a ceremony but an on-going commitment. Each day, for the rest of our lives, we will make choices. We will choose whether to be faithful, whether to be kind and patient with each other. We will choose whether to find fault or whether to be forgiving.

In the days and years ahead, we will have to choose, again and again, whether or not to keep our love as the most important part of our lives.

I chose you as my life's partner and I promise now to make our love my on-going choice.

Twenty

I believe in the power of love. I believe that love is the single most potent force in the universe. It is the source of all joy, the unifying strength which links spirit to spirit. The capacity to love is our great chance for happiness.

On this wonderful day, my heart overflows with feelings of love. I love my family and my friends; I love all of the people who came to witness this wedding.

Most of all, I love you, (name). I believe so strongly in love's great power that I now promise to spend the rest of my lifetime with you.

Chapter Six

Vows in Dialogue Form

Groom: Today we cross an invisible line.

Bride: We leave behind our yesterdays and start our lives anew.

Groom: The past is over. We will concern ourselves only with the future.

Bride: It is a new day, a new commitment, a new life.

Groom: The vows we take today will change us forever.

Bride: I take them gladly.

Groom: I take them gladly, too.

Bride: (Name), I promise to love you, to protect you, and to be faithful to you for all the days of my life. I will soothe your hurts and share your delights. I will do all in my power to make you as happy as I am today.

Groom: (Name), I promise to love you and honor you and to always be honest with you. I will be faithful to you for all the days of my life. I will believe only the best about you and look always for your good qualities. I will do all in my power to make you as happy as I am today.

Bride: Today is the beginning of the rest of my life. I choose to spend today, and all of my tomorrows, with you.

Groom: Today is the beginning of the rest of my life. I choose to spend it, and all of my tomorrows, with you.

Groom: I love you, (*Name*).

Bride: I love you, (*Name*).

Groom: I want you for my wife, that we may share our lives with each other.

Bride: I want you for my husband, that our love may be sanctified by this ceremony.

Groom: I promise to put you first in my life, knowing that our love is my most precious possession.

Bride: I promise to put you first in my life, believing that all other achievements pale beside a happy marriage.

Groom: I will share with you my joys, my sorrows, my hopes and my dreams.

Bride: I will bring to you my accomplishments and my failures.

Groom: I will be faithful to you always.

Bride: And I will be faithful to you.

Groom: From this day forward, I will walk beside you. When we are apart, my thoughts will be with you.

Bride: From this day forward, we stand together. Whatever happens to either of us will be confronted by both.

Groom: I gladly make these promises. I am proud to be your husband.

Bride: I gladly make these promises. I am proud to be your wife.

Groom: Our vows are ended; our marriage has begun.

Bride: Let us go with joy into our new life together.

Groom: This is a day of rejoicing.

Bride: We rejoice in the goodness of love.

Groom: Because I love you, I promise to respect your wishes and opinions.

Bride: Because I love you, I promise to put our marriage above all else.

Groom: I will share with you my material goods, my thoughts, and my feelings.

Bride: I will share with you my material goods, my thoughts, and my feelings.

Groom: I promise to do all that I can to keep our relationship special to both of us.

Bride: I will cherish our time together. I will try to keep our home peaceful and harmonious.

Groom: I will encourage you to grow and to become all that you are capable of becoming.

Bride: I will urge you to meet whatever challenges you may face.

Groom: I promise to be faithful to you in thought, word, and act.

Bride: I promise to be faithful to you in thought, word, and act. This is a day of rejoicing.

Groom: We rejoice in the goodness of love.

Officiate: Marriage is not a legal document. No pastor or priest or justice of the peace can create a marriage because a marriage, truly, is nothing except the promises made and kept by two individuals. Today (*Man's name*) and (*Woman's name*) stand before us to publicly declare their love and to share with us their marriage promises. (*Man's name*), what promises do you make?

Groom: I promise to love (*Woman's name*) with all my heart and mind and strength. I promise to be faithful to her in thought, word and act for all the days of my life. I promise to consider her welfare and happiness before I make any decisions and I promise to offer her comfort, encouragement and companionship.

Officiate: (*Woman's name*), what promises do you make?

Bride: I promise to love (*Man's name*) with all my heart and mind and strength. I promise to be faithful to him in thought, word and act for all the days of my life. I promise to consider his welfare and happiness before I make any decisions and I promise to offer him comfort, encouragement and companionship.

Officiate: Do you both, before these witnesses, pledge to do all in your power to make this a happy and enduring union?

Together: We do.

(Rose Ceremony)

NOTE: The groom will need to have a rose and the bride will need a bud vase with water in it. Before the ceremony, the vase and rose should be placed in an easily accessible spot — behind a lectern, for example. The best man, the maid of honor, or the officiate should get the rose and the vase just prior to this part of the service.

Officiate: This is a day steeped in tradition, a time when we are surrounded by symbols: something old, something new, something borrowed, something blue.

Today, (*Bride's name*) and (*Groom's name*) begin a new tradition, a custom which now becomes uniquely their own.

Groom: (*Bride's name*), I give you this rose. Because it grew from a tiny seed, becoming stronger and larger until it burst into flower, it symbolizes the way my love for you has grown. (*He gives her the rose.*) Each year on our wedding anniversary, I will give you another rose. In so doing, I'll remember this day and renew the vows we've made.

Bride: (*Groom's name*), I give to you this vase of water. (*He takes and holds it.*) Because water is the one element without which we would perish, it symbolizes the importance of your love in my life. Each year on our anniversary, I will refill this vase, offering it to you as a symbol of my ever renewing love. (*She puts the rose in the vase and they hold the vase together.*)

Groom: Without water, the rose would die.

Bride: Without the rose, the vase of water would not be

beautiful.

Groom: My gift is enhanced by yours, just as my life is enhanced by yours.

Bride: My gift is lovely because of yours, just as my life is better because of you. (*They hand the rose and vase to the officiate.*)

Officiate: On each anniversary, as you give and receive the rose and the water, remember with joy this day when you pledged your love and your lives to each other.

May this be only the first of many cherished traditions in a home filled with happiness.

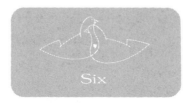

Groom: Today is a new beginning. It is the start of a new way of life.

Bride: We don't know what challenges lie ahead. We know only that we will face them together.

Groom: Because of you, I am a better person than I once was.

Bride: I promise always to see the good in you.

Groom: I will try to be worthy of your love and trust.

Bride: Because of you, I am a better person than I once was.

Groom: I promise always to see the good in you.

Bride: I will try to be worthy of your love and trust.

Groom: Before God and these witnesses, I vow to be loyal to you in every way, to comfort you, to cherish you, and always to love you.

Bride: Before God and these witnesses, I vow to be loyal to you in every way, to comfort you, to cherish you, and always to love you.

Groom: Today is a new beginning.

Bride: Our new life together has begun.

Groom: Love is more than an emotion. It is a way of life.

Bride: Love is more than a feeling. It is a channel through which all feelings flow.

Groom: When I offer you my love, I offer all that is important in my life.

Bride: When I offer you my love, I let all of my deepest feelings flow toward you.

Groom: Marriage is more than a ceremony. This service lasts less than an hour but marriage is a lifetime of living together.

Bride: Marriage is more than a promise. It is a promise kept; it is words translated into action.

Groom: As we begin living our promises, I pledge to you my love and loyalty. I will share with you all that is important to me. I will encourage peace and happiness between us.

Bride: As we begin living our promises, I pledge to you my love and loyalty. I will share with you all that is important to me. I will encourage peace and happiness between us.

Eight

Bride: I, (*Name*), take you, (*Name*), to be my husband. I promise to be true to you always, in sickness and in health, in poverty or wealth, in my thoughts and in my speaking. I will be your dearest friend, your lover, and the mother of your children. With these vows, I commit myself to you.

Groom: I, (*Name*), take you, (*Name*), to be my wife. I promise to be true to you always, in sickness and in health, in poverty or wealth, in my thoughts and in my speaking. I will be your dearest friend, your lover, and the father of your children. With these vows, I commit myself to you.

Nine

Officiate: Marriage is an act of faith. It requires great trust to pledge oneself to a lifetime with another person. Today (*Name*) and (*Name*) demonstrate their faith and trust by pledging their love to each other.

    (*Bride's name*), what promises do you make to (*Groom's name*)?

Bride: (*Name*), I affirm you now as my life partner. I promise to stay with you in times of celebration and in times of mourning. I promise to love you, honor you, and be faithful to you. I accept you, without reservation, as my husband.

Officiate: (*Groom's name*), what promises do you make to (*Bride's name*)?

Groom: (*Name*), I affirm you now as my life partner. I promise to stay with you in times of celebration and in times of mourning. I promise to love you, honor you, and be faithful to you. I accept you, without reservation, as my wife.

Officiate: By the promises they've made, (*Name*) and (*Name*) have demonstrated their belief in love, in marriage, and in each other. They ask now for the blessing of all who have witnessed their vows. If you believe in their love and approve their marriage, please applaud.

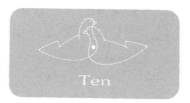

Ten

Groom: I promise to live in such a way that I will never
bring dishonor or heartache into our marriage.
Bride: I promise to keep our home a sanctuary of love,
contentment and compassionate understanding.
Groom: I pledge to you my patience, my honesty, and my
faith in the rightness of our love.
Bride: I pledge to you my patience, my honesty, and my
faith in the rightness of our love.
Groom: To the best of my ability, I will be your friend, your
helpmate, your counselor and your sweetheart.
Bride: To the best of my ability, I will be your friend, your
helpmate, your counselor and your sweetheart.
Groom: I love you and I want to be your husband.
Bride: I love you and I want to be your wife.

Eleven

Officiate: You are different people today than you were five years ago. Five years from now, you will be different still. Yet, you are about to make promises which are meant to last a lifetime. May you grant each other the gift of growth.

Groom: (*Bride's name*), I expect you to change, just as I will change. My promise to you is that, as I grow, I will share the growth with you.

Bride: I will not expect you always to think and believe exactly as you do today. I will encourage your growth and you will encourage mine. I promise to respect your opinions even when they differ from my own.

Groom: I promise to respect your opinions even when they differ from my own.

Bride: I will be your partner but never your shadow.

Groom: I will be your equal but not your double.

Bride: I will bring to you my ideas and interests, not expecting you always to have the same enthusiasms.

Groom: Our separate interests will keep our friendship from becoming stagnant.

Bride: I will strive for a love that is flexible, that adapts to your changing needs.

Groom: I will strive for a love that is flexible, that adapts to your changing needs.

Officiate: I offer you the good wishes of myself and this congregation. As your love grows, may you also grow in the capacity to share it. May every change bring you increased happiness.

Twelve

Together: We believe in love.
Bride: I believe in love's ability to accept.
Groom: I believe in love's capacity to forgive.
Bride: I will accept you as you are. I will forgive you if you
    fail.
Groom: I will accept you as you are and forgive you if you
    fail.
Bride: Love demands respect but not obedience.
Groom: Love requires loyalty without subservience. I
    promise to respect you as my equal and to be loyal
    to you in every way.
Bride: I promise to respect you as my equal and to be loyal
    to you in every way.
Together: We believe in love.

Thirteen

Groom: Love thrives on honesty. I promise always to be truthful with you.

Bride: Love is nourished by thoughtfulness. I promise that my actions will reflect my high regard for you.

Groom: I believe that the power of love can change lives. My life is changed because I love you.

Bride: Love can bring joy, hope and strength. Our love has brought all of those to me.

Groom: I promise that the home we are founding today will have love at its core. I will do all that I can to nourish and enrich our love for each other.

Bride: I promise that the home we are founding today will have love at its core. I will do all that I can to nourish and enrich our love for each other.

Bride: When I felt empty inside, you poured your love into my hollow heart and made me whole. Now, my cup runneth over; my heart overflows with gladness.

Groom: When my frightened soul shed tears of loneliness, you offered me your love and the shadows disappeared. For all the gladness of this day, I thank you.

Bride: For all the years ahead, I rejoice.

Groom: I pledge to you now my love for all time and I ask you to be my wife.

Bride: I accept gladly. I pledge to you now my love for all time and I ask you to be my husband.

Groom: I accept gladly.

Bride: I love you for looking at me and seeing only the best.

Groom: I love you for listening to me and hearing only the good. I will strive to become what you think I am.

Bride: In our times together, I promise to see you always through the eyes of love.

Groom: In our times together, I promise to see you always through the eyes of love.

Sixteen

Bride: I never meant to love so much. I meant to keep my emotions under control because I didn't want to be vulnerable.

Groom: I never meant to love so much. I intended to be rational and calm.

Bride: I thought I could care, but within boundaries.

Groom: I thought I could love, but with limitations.

Bride: I meant to let you be one part of my life; instead you have become more important than life itself.

Groom: I meant to keep our love in its own compartment; instead it has overflowed the boundaries into everything I say and do and feel.

Bride: I meant to be cautious.

Groom: I meant to stay uncommitted.

Bride: Now, because I do care so much, I am vulnerable. And I do not mind.

Groom: I joyfully accept the commitments of marriage.

Bride: From this day forward, I promise to love you willingly and completely, withholding nothing.

Groom: From this day forward, I promise to love you willingly and completely, withholding nothing.

Bride: I never meant to love so much, but it has happened. And I am glad.

Groom: It has happened. And I am glad.

Seventeen

Bride: You came softly into my heart, drifting gently as a fluff of dandelion floats on the summer breeze. You came softly into my heart and made me your own.

Groom: You crept slowly into my life, moving quietly, as the clouds slide past the moon on a winter's eve. You crept slowly into my life, and made me your own.

Bride: You have changed my life forever. Because you love me, I see with new eyes and hear with new ears. I delight in every day.

Groom: You have changed my life forever. Because you love me, I find joy in each awakening. My senses are alive with the wonder of your love.

Bride: I promise now to keep my heart ever open to you. I will love you, stand beside you, and wish only the best for you. I will be faithful to you always.

Groom: I promise now to keep my heart ever open to you. I will love you, stand beside you, and wish only the best for you. I will be faithful to you always.

Eighteen

Groom: I take you, (*Name*), to be my wife. I join with you to share all that is to come.

Bride: I take you, (*Name*), to be my husband. I join with you to share all that is to come.

Groom: I will be faithful to you as long as God gives us life together. Each rising sun will find you by my side.

Bride: I will be faithful to you as long as God gives us life together. Each rising sun will find you by my side.

Groom: I will treasure our new life above all else.

Bride: I will treasure our new life above all else. All that I am, and all that I ever hope to be, is yours.

Groom: All that I am, and all that I ever hope to be, is yours.

Nineteen

Groom: We are not two half-people who are about to become one whole person.
Bride: We are two whole people, who come together in joy for the fulfillment of life.
Groom: I pledge to you my love. Together, we will bear life's burdens without self-pity or flight.
Bride: I pledge to you my love. Together, we will welcome life's blessings with gladness and thanksgiving.
Groom: I will be a friend to you.
Bride: I will be your biggest fan.
Groom: I love you; I ask you to accept me as your husband.
Bride: I love you and accept you gladly. Will you accept me as your wife?
Groom: I will.

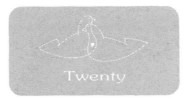

Twenty

Bride: I come to you in love. I feel humble, knowing that you trust me enough to share the rest of your life with me.

Groom: I come to you in love. I feel honored, knowing that you trust me enough to share the rest of your life with me.

Bride: Any mistakes of the past are behind us; we start today with a clean slate.

Groom: We put behind us our separate lives and begin our new life together.

Bride: I will do all that I can to ensure that our life together is fulfilling for both of us.

Groom: I will do all that I can to ensure that we continue to find happiness with each other.

Bride: I come to you in love. I will stay with you, in love, for all the days of my life.

Groom: I come to you in love. I will stay with you, in love, for all the days of my life.

Chapter Seven

Ring
Ceremonies

Groom: (*Name*), I give you this ring as a symbol of my love. As it encircles your finger, may it remind you always that you are surrounded by my enduring love.

Bride: I will wear it gladly. Whenever I look at it, I will remember this joyous day and the vows we've made. (*Name*), I give you this ring as a symbol of my love. As it encircles your finger, may it remind you always that you are surrounded by my enduring love.

Groom: I will wear it gladly. Whenever I look at it, I will remember this joyous day and the vows we've made.

Groom: I have for you a golden ring. The precious metal symbolizes that your love is the most precious element in my life. The ring has no beginning and no ending, which symbolizes that the love between us will never cease. I place it on your finger as a visible sign of the vows which have made us husband and wife.

Bride: I have for you a golden ring. The precious metal symbolizes that I value your love above all else. The ring goes endlessly on, just as our love will endure forever. I place it on your finger as a symbol of the vows which have made us husband and wife.

25

Three

Bride: Please give me your hand. (*He does; she puts the ring on his finger.*) I give you now this wedding ring, a symbol of my unending love and devotion. May its presence on your hand serve always to remind you of my love.

Groom: I will wear it proudly. Please give me your hand. (*She does; he puts the ring on her finger.*) I give you now this wedding ring, a symbol of my unending love and devotion. May its presence on your hand remind you of my love.

Bride: I will wear it proudly.

Four

Groom: With this ring, I wed you — for today, for tomorrow and for all the years to come. Please wear it as a sign of my love and a notice to all the world that you have chosen me to be your husband.

Bride: With this ring, I wed you — for today, for tomorrow and for all the years to come. Please wear it as a sign of my love and a notice to all the world that you have chosen me to be your wife.

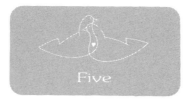

Bride: I give you this ring as an emblem of my love. It signifies that our souls are joined in life-long ties.

Groom: I give you this ring as an emblem of my love. It signifies that our souls are joined in life-long ties.

Bride: This ring is beautiful — shining and pure. I will strive to keep our marriage beautiful, too.

Groom: This ring is hard — sturdy and strong. I will strive to keep our marriage strong, too.

Groom: Because this ring is perfectly symmetrical, it signifies the perfection of true love. As I place it on your finger, I give you all that I am and ever hope to be.

Bride: Because this ring has no end or beginning, it signifies the continuation of true love. As I place it on your finger, I give you all that I am and ever hope to be.

Seven

Groom: (*Name*), I have brought you a ring, the age-old symbol of love and fidelity. With it, I offer you my heart and soul as your husband. Will you accept?

Bride: I accept with joy. (*He places the ring on her finger.*)

Groom: May its presence on your finger be a constant reminder of my love.

Bride: (*Name*), I have brought you a ring, the age-old symbol of love and fidelity. With it, I offer you my heart and soul as your wife. Will you accept?

Groom: I accept with joy. (*She places the ring on his finger.*)

Bride: May its presence on your finger be a constant reminder of my love.

Groom: I give you now this ring and with it I give you my love.

Bride: I accept the ring; I accept your love.

Groom: The ring is symbolic of all that is in my heart today. When you wear it, know that you are wearing an emblem of my love.

Bride: I give you now this ring and with it I give you my love.

Groom: I accept the ring; I accept your love.

Bride: Just as the ring encircles your finger, going endlessly on, so will my love for you continue, year after year.

Groom: With this ring, I thee wed. I accept thee as my wife. I endow thee with all my worldly goods. I acknowledge thee as my partner throughout the rest of my life. Thou art my beloved.

Bride: With this ring, I thee wed. I accept thee as my husband. I endow thee with all my worldly goods. I acknowledge thee as my partner throughout the rest of my life. Thou art my beloved.

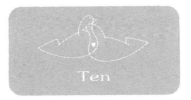

Ten

Officiate: (*Name*), what do you bring as enduring evidence of your sincerity?
Groom: I have brought a ring, the best known symbol of love and marriage. (*He puts it on bride's finger.*) It will serve as a visible reminder of my constant love and the promises we've just made.
Officiate: (*Name*), what do you bring as enduring evidence of your sincerity?
Bride: I also have brought a ring, symbolizing the infinity of love. (*She puts it on the groom's finger.*) May its presence on your finger remind you always of my love and of the promises we've made today.
Officiate: Through the giving and receiving of these rings, your life-long pact is sealed.

Eleven

Groom: The vows we've made are invisible; the love we
  feel is invisible, too.
Bride: Our marriage is a joining of two spirits, a merging of
  our innermost souls.
Groom: (*Name*) and I desire to have a visible, material
  sign of these inward and spiritual ties. We've chosen
  rings as the symbols we wish to wear.
Bride: When we give and receive these rings, we signify
  the giving and receiving of love. (*They exchange
  rings.*)
Groom: Each day, as I wear this ring, I will renew the vows
  I've made.
Bride: Each day, as I wear this ring, I will renew the vows
  I've made.

Chapter Eight

Special Vows

Thank You to the Parents

Groom: (*Name bride's parents*), would you please stand? (*Bride's parents stand.*)

Groom: Thank you for raising (*bride's name*) to be the woman of my dreams. Thank you for the love and care which have made her so special. I ask you to accept me now as your son.

Bride's parents: We welcome you into our family. (*They sit.*)

Bride: (*Name groom's parents*), would you please stand? (*Groom's parents stand.*)

Bride: Thank you for raising (*Groom's name*) to be the man I choose to spend my life with. Thank you for the love and care which have made him so special. I ask you to accept me now as your daughter.

Groom's parents: We welcome you into our family. (*They sit.*)

Bride: Before we say our vows, we want to thank our parents for all that they have done for us.

Groom: We learned how to love because we were raised in loving homes.

Bride: We feel secure and confident in our love because our parents allowed us to be independent. They are the wind beneath our wings.

Groom: They have shown us, by example, what a happy marriage can be.

Bride: Thanks, Mom and Dad.

Groom: Thanks, Mom and Dad.

Groom: We thank everyone for coming today. Your presence makes this ceremony more meaningful for us.

Bride: We especially want to thank our parents — not just for being here today, but for being there for us so many times in the past.

Groom: Although we are founding a new home, the love we feel for the homes of our childhood will continue.

Addendum
To be used, if desired, at the conclusion of any ceremony

Bride: For each of us, a few bright days stand out above the rest. This day, this hour, is the brightest of my life.

Groom: It is a golden moment, made splendid by love.

Bride: I know that all our days together will not be as glorious as this one. There must always be valleys between the mountain peaks.

Groom: When we find ourselves in a valley, we will remember this day. We will recall this shining hour and the feelings of tenderness we share. The memory will help us through any problems.

Bride: Today is the fulfillment of our dearest dream.

Groom: Together we will create new dreams.

Bride: This ceremony is the culmination of many months of planning. Yet it is not the end; it is only the beginning.

Groom: We have said our vows, we have made our promises, we have pledged our love.

Bride: We will carry these words in our memories and these moments in our hearts forever.

Five

A Vow Which Includes the Child/Children of the Bride or Groom

Groom: I have pledged my love and promised to be a faithful husband. Now I want to add another, different kind of vow. I promise to love (*name of bride's child*) and to treat him/her as if he/she were my own. I gladly accept the obligations that go along with this pledge. I love (*child's name*) and want him/her to be a part of my life.

or

Bride: I have pledged my love and promised to be a faithful wife. Now I want to add another, different kind of vow. I promise to love (*name of groom's child*) and to treat him/her as if he/she were my own. I gladly accept the obligations that go along with this pledge. I love (*child's name*) and want him/her to be a part of my life.

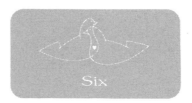

(If desired, the officiate can invite the bride's and groom's children, by name, to stand.)

Groom: Just as I love (*bride's name*), I also love her children. (*Name*) and (*name*), I promise you, before all of these witnesses, that I will be a loving stepfather. I anticipate with joy many happy times together. I welcome you into my heart and home.

Bride: Just as I love (*groom's name*), I also love his son/ daughter. (*Name*), I promise you, before all of these witnesses, that I will be a loving stepmother. I anticipate with joy many happy times together. I welcome you into my heart and home.

Chapter Nine

Anniversary
Vows

Anniversary Vows

The vows in this chapter are intended for use during the celebration of a wedding anniversary. Some couples repeat their wedding vows each year on their anniversary, as a way to renew their love and repledge their fidelity. Other couples use special anniversary vows for milestone anniversaries or for those anniversaries which are celebrated with other people. Parties to honor couples on their anniversary are most common for the 10th, the 25th or the 50th anniversary.

Anniversary vows can be used in private or public. They can be the highlight of a family gathering, or a secret tender exchange between husband and wife.

Like the wedding vows in this book, the anniversary vows are meant to be examples. They can be used as is, or they can be the basis for writing personalized vows.

If you want to write your own anniversary vows, follow the instructions in Chapter Four. You should read all of the sample wedding vows in this book, as well as the anniversary vows which follow. Many of the phrases in the wedding vows can be adapted to anniversary vows.

Wife: How little we knew of love, my love.

Husband: How little we knew of love.

Wife: We knew of movie love and book love. We saw other marriages and thought we knew what love is.

Husband: But we really didn't know anything at all.

Wife: We have learned, you and I. We have learned how to love.

Husband: The learning has been a splendid process.

Wife: I have learned that a choice, once made, is not necessarily finished. I have chosen you many times since our wedding day. I choose you still.

Husband: I have learned that a love once formed is never wholly complete. My love for you grows daily.

Wife: How little we knew of love, my love. How much more we know of love now.

Husband: Do you suppose, some years from now, we'll look back on *this* day and say, "How little we knew of love?"

Husband: Today I remember our wedding. I celebrate the joy I felt that day and the many happy times we've had together since then.

Wife: I thank you for living up to my expectations. On our wedding day, I hoped that our years together would be filled with contentment and mutual respect. My hopes have materialized.

Husband: On our wedding day, I dreamed of sharing my life with you so that we both would be enriched by the sharing. The dreams I cherished for us have come true.

Wife: As we enter another year of marriage, I renew the promises that I made (*number*) years ago.

Husband: As we enter another year of marriage, I renew the promises that I made (*number*) years ago.

Wife: I loved you then. I love you more now.

Husband: I loved you then. I love you more now.

Three

On our wedding day, I made a choice. It was the most important choice of my life. On that day, I chose you to be my husband/wife.

I thought then that such a decision, once made, was final. Now I know that the selection of a life partner is not a one-time decision but an on-going process. Many times in the years since then, I have chosen you again.

The reason is simple: no other person has ever made me this happy. No one else brings me such joy.

I want to stay with you for the rest of my life — not because I feel obligated to meet your needs but because you continue to meet mine. I live with you not because a legal document says I am your wife/husband but because, in my heart of hearts, I want to be by your side more than I want to be anywhere else.

On our wedding day, I made a choice. I make it still.

Four

Husband: How young we were, (number) years ago.
Wife: How much we've learned since then.
Husband: We've learned that not all dreams are attainable.
Wife: We've learned that people grow and change.
Husband: We've learned that we can't always control the forces which have an impact on our lives.
Wife: The hurts have been deeper than we expected and the joys have been greater.
Husband: The pleasures have far outweighed the disappointments.
Wife: If I could go back and do it over again, I would still marry you.
Husband: If I could go back and do it over again, I would still marry you.
Wife: When we got married, I thought I loved you. Now I know I do.
Husband: When we got married, I thought I loved you. Now I know I do.

Five

25th Anniversary

Twenty-five years! We have changed since then and the world around us has changed, too. But one thing has not changed: our love for each other.

Twenty-five years ago, I promised to love you, to give of my best to you, to cherish and keep you no matter what happened.

I have not always lived up to my best intentions, but I have always loved you. I still love you. I love you even more now than I did then because I know you better. Age and maturity have increased my capacity for love and my pleasure in it.

We've watched our babies grow up and become independent. We've moved. We've had set-backs and successes. We've weathered a good many storms.

Through all of it, the one constant in our lives, our love, has grown stronger.

It is with a glad heart that I renew my original wedding vows. I still promise to love you, honor you, cherish and keep you. I continue to want you, for better or worse, for richer or poorer.

Whatever the future may hold for us, we will always have our love. It is enough.

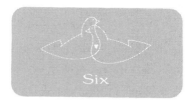

Six

25th Anniversary

Wife: After twenty-five years, you are still my dearest
friend.

Husband: After twenty-five years, you are still the woman
of my dreams.

Wife: I thank you for the happiness of our time together.
Thank you for your patience, your support, your
caring.

Husband: I thank you for the joy our marriage has brought
me. Thank you for your understanding, your
gentleness, your willingness to overlook mistakes.

Wife: It seems like only yesterday that we pledged our love.

Husband: I pledge it again today. I love you and I hope
we'll be blessed with twenty-five more years
together.

Wife: I love you, too, and I pledge my love again today.

50th Anniversary

Husband: We promised to love for better and for worse, and we have done it.

Wife: Our love has made the good times better and the bad times bearable.

Husband: We promised to love for richer and for poorer, and it has happened. We've known plentiful times and lean times; we have loved through both.

Wife: We promised to love in sickness and in health, and we have done so. We have been strong and we have been weak; we've each had our turn to take care of the other. We have given and received comfort.

Husband: Fifty years ago, we promised to spend our lifetimes together. We were filled with hopes and dreams and youthful anticipation. Today I thank you for making those hopes and dreams come true.

Wife: Thank you for the years of joy; for the laughter and the hugs; for the unfailing, supportive love.

Husband: We promised to love and we have kept our promise.

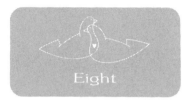

Eight

50th Aniversary

Wife: We are here for a celebration.

Husband: We are here to celebrate love.

Wife: We are here to celebrate marriage — our own specific marriage which has endured for fifty years.

Husband: Today we commemorate those fifty years. We rejoice that fifty years ago we had the good sense to marry each other.

Wife: We have dried each other's tears; we have applauded each other's successes. For fifty years, we have lived and loved together.

Husband: Today we applaud the memory of all those years. We celebrate, as well, the hopes we cherish for the years ahead. Most of all, we celebrate this moment, today, this special once-in-a-lifetime occasion which our love has earned for us.

Wife: Today is a day of days, a time of times, a dream come true. Like all the other days of our lives, we celebrate it together.

Anniversary Vows Done As a Reading
By Someone Else

Sometimes a couple prefers to have someone else read the anniversary vows for them. Especially if many guests are present to celebrate a special anniversary, the honored couple may feel too nervous to say the anniversary vows themselves. A nice alternative is to ask one of their children or grandchildren to give such a special reading.

The words will be just as meaningful when done this way and the honored couple may feel more relaxed and able to enjoy the festivities if they don't have to "perform."

The two Fiftieth Annniversary vows lend themselves nicely to this kind of adaptation. They are printed now in that form, as an alternative way to use them.

Alternate Version

(*Name*) and (*Name*) promised to love for better and for worse, and they have done it. Their love has made the good times better and the bad times bearable.

They promised to love for richer and for poorer, and it has happened. They've known plentiful times and lean times; they have loved through both.

They promised to love in sickness and in health, and they have done so. They have been strong and they have been weak. They have each had a turn to take care of the other. They have given and received comfort.

Fifty years ago, (*Name*) and (*Name*) promised to spend their lifetimes together. They were filled with hopes and dreams and youthful anticipation. Today they celebrate the fact that those hopes and dreams came true.

They are glad for their years of joy; for the laughter and hugs; for the unfailing, supportive love.

Fifty years ago, (*Name*) and (*name*) promised to love. They have kept their promise.

Alternate Version

We are here for a celebration. We are here to celebrate love. We are here to celebrate marriage — one, specific marriage between (*Name*) and (*Name*) which has endured for fifty years.

Today we commemorate those fifty years. We rejoice that a half century ago, (*Name*) and (*Name*) had the good sense to marry each other.

They have dried each other's tears and applauded each other's successes. For fifty years, they have lived and loved together.

We each cherish certain memories from this wonderful marriage. We honor those memories and we hope that (*Name*) and (*Name*) will have many more happy years together.

Most of all, we celebrate this moment, today, this once-in-a-lifetime occasion which love has created. Today is a day of days, a time of times, a dream come true. Happy anniversary.

PHOTO CREDITS

ABOUT THE AUTHOR
PEG KEHRET

After years of anonymity writing radio commercials and advertising blurbs, Peg Kehret expanded into the total craft of wordsmithery. She began putting her name to articles, light verse, short stories, situation comedies and educational scripts. She has published both fiction and nonfiction books and hundreds of short stories and magazine articles.

She has published over 200 pieces in such periodicals as *Catholic Digest, Good Housekeeping, Modern Bride, The Reader's Digest, The Wall Street Journal* and *The Writer.*

Peg lives with her husband and an assortment of pets in an 80-year-old farmhouse near Redmond, Washington, a suburb of Seattle.